Do-it-yourself

POWERS OF ATTORNEY & LIVING WILL

LAW PACK™ GUIDE

Powers of Attorney and Living Will Guide

First edition 1997
Second edition 2000
Third edition 2001

Law Pack Publishing Limited
10-16 Cole Street
London SE1 4YH

www.lawpack.co.uk

Printed in Great Britain

ISBN: 1 902646 69 X

Important facts

This Law Pack Guide contains the information, instruction and forms necessary to create an Enduring Power of Attorney, a General Power of Attorney and a Living Will without a solicitor. This Guide is for use in England or Wales. It is not suitable for use in Scotland or Northern Ireland.

The information it contains has been carefully compiled from professional sources, but its accuracy is not guaranteed, as laws and regulations may change or be subject to differing interpretations.

Neither this nor any other publication can take the place of a solicitor on important legal matters. As with any legal matter, common sense should determine whether you need the assistance of a solicitor rather than rely solely on the information and forms in this Law Pack Guide.

We strongly urge you to consult a solicitor if:

- substantial amounts of money are involved;
- you do not understand the instructions or are uncertain how to complete and use a form correctly;
- what you want to do is not precisely covered by the this Guide.

Exclusion of Liability and Disclaimer

This book is sold with the understanding that neither the author nor the publisher is engaged in rendering legal advice. If legal advice is required, the services of a solicitor should be sought. The publisher and the author cannot in any way guarantee that the forms in this book are being used for the purposes intended and, therefore, assume no responsibility for their proper and correct use.

Whilst every effort has been made to ensure that this Law Pack Guide provides accurate and expert guidance, it is impossible to predict all the circumstances in which it may be used. Accordingly, the publisher, author, distributor, retailer and the solicitor who has approved the contents shall not be liable to any person or entity with respect to any loss or damage caused or alleged to be caused directly or indirectly by what is contained in or left out of this Law Pack Guide.

Table of contents

How to use this Law Pack Guide

This Law Pack Guide can help you achieve an important legal objective conveniently, efficiently and economically. Remember that it is important for you to use this guide properly if you are to avoid later difficulties.

Step-by-step instructions for using this guide:

1. Read this guide carefully. If after thorough examination you decide that your requirements are not met by this Law Pack Guide, or you do not feel confident about writing your own documents, consult a solicitor.

2. At the end of this guide there are completed examples of the forms needed to handle your own Enduring Power of Attorney, General Power of Attorney and Living Will and template forms for photocopying and use.

3. Set the photocopier to expand by 122% to produce full-sized copies, and make several copies of the original forms for practice and future use. You should also make copies of the completed forms. Create a record-keeping system for both sets of copies.

4. When completing a form, do not leave any section blank. If any section is inapplicable, write 'not applicable' or 'none'. This shows you have not overlooked the section.

5. Always use a pen or type on legal documents; never use pencil.

6. Do not cross out or erase anything you have written on your final forms.

7. You will find a helpful glossary of terms at the end of this Law Pack Guide. Refer to this glossary if you find unfamiliar terms.

8. Always keep legal documents in a safe place and in a location known to your spouse, family, executor or solicitor.

Introduction

Asking somebody to do something for you is an everyday matter: you ask a friend to pick up your dry cleaning or post your letters. But if you want someone to act on your behalf on more weighty matters with full legal authority, so they can buy and sell your shares for example, the law requires and provides a means for doing this: a 'power of attorney'.

If the power of attorney is to be on a long-term basis complications arise in the event of the person giving the power becoming mentally 'incapacitated'. This could happen either because of old age or serious illness. And as medical knowledge and life expectancy advance it is becoming more and more important to plan for a time when you may not be able to make decisions for yourself. This Guide tells you how you can most effectively protect your assets should you become unable to communicate your wishes in the future, by creating an 'enduring' power of attorney.

This Guide also helps you identify the means through which you can indicate your preferences in the vital matter of health care, by means of a written Living Will. It contains information on current laws and where no laws yet exist, the most accepted and effective practice.

What is a Power of Attorney?

Highlight

A power of attorney is the formal, written authority granted by one person (the 'Donor') to another person (the 'Attorney') enabling the Attorney to act on the Donor's behalf and manage his or her financial interests.

A power of attorney is the formal, written authority granted by one person (the 'Donor') to another person (the 'Attorney') enabling the Attorney to act on the Donor's behalf and manage his or her financial interests.

This Guide deals with two kinds of power of attorney: General and Enduring. A General Power of Attorney is a relatively straightforward authorisation for wide-ranging use for specific periods or events. The need to create a General Power might arise, for example, if you go abroad and need to entrust the management of business interests to your spouse.

Enduring Powers of Attorney (EPAs) are rather more complicated to create and administer than General Powers for the simple reason that they remain valid in the event of the Donor becoming mentally incapable of handling his or her own affairs, and so require particular procedures and formalities to be followed. A General Power on the other hand is automatically revoked if the Donor becomes mentally incapable.

The actual scope and nature of an Attorney's power under an EPA and a General Power are broadly the same, except that an EPA can define and restrict the authority given whereas a General Power cannot. An EPA provides a way of allowing there to be long-term control of a Donor's interests, albeit in the hands of others, particularly if he or she is elderly or in poor health.

This Guide contains a General Power form and instructions for its completion in chapter 6. The other chapters in the first half of this Guide deal solely with aspects of creating and administering an EPA.

How Enduring Powers of Attorney are different ━━━━━━━━━━━━

Unlike a General Power, an EPA remains effective *after* the Donor has become mentally incapable of managing his or her own affairs.

To be valid an EPA must have been granted by the Donor while he or she was still mentally capable. When the Attorney believes the Donor is or may soon become incapable, he or she must:

1) Give notice to the Donor of his or her intention to apply to register the EPA with an office of the Supreme Court called the Court of Protection (the role of the Court of Protection, as defined by the Mental Health Act 1983, is to safeguard the property and affairs of people with mental disability).

2) Give notice of his or her intention to certain of the Donor's nearest relatives.

3) Apply to the Court of Protection to register the EPA.

Until the EPA is registered and full power is restored, the Attorney will have limited authority. Please refer to chapter 5 for a detailed discussion on the registration procedure.

The benefits of an Enduring Power of Attorney ━━━━━━━━━━

If you were to become ill or disabled without an EPA and were unable to manage your financial affairs yourself, no one could act on your behalf unless he or she first went to court and was appointed your Receiver by the Court of Protection. Even your spouse and children would be powerless to act on your behalf. Although courts will appoint someone to act for you and to protect your interests, this is not always a desirable alternative for three reasons:

1) **The delay**. It can take several weeks or even months to have someone appointed who will have the authority to make legal, financial and business decisions for the Donor. With an EPA the Attorney can act for the Donor immediately. The continued control of your interests is thus maintained by someone you have chosen.

2) **Selection of Attorney**. When someone is ill or disabled they lose the ability to select their Attorney. The court may or may not appoint as Receiver the person the Donor would have preferred.

3) **Advantages of immediate and lasting delegation.** From the date on which the EPA is signed by the Attorney (see chapter 3), he or she has authority to act on behalf of the Donor unless this power has been specifically excluded by the Donor. This means that the Donor can take advantage of being able to delegate responsibilities if, for example, he or she goes on holiday.

Must the EPA be in a particular form?

Yes. The form of an EPA differs significantly from the relatively simple wording of a General Power. The Enduring Powers of Attorney (Prescribed Form) Regulations 1990 require that all EPAs follow a specific form, as contained in this Guide (see pages 54–57 for a completed example). The form must include explanatory information which you will see in Part A and in all the relevant marginal notes to parts B and C. You should read this information carefully.

The notes included in the EPA form are designed to make clear to both the Donor and the Attorney the extent and nature of the Attorney's powers and duties. This is particularly important because the Attorney has a duty to register the EPA as soon as it becomes clear that the Donor is, or will soon be, incapable of acting on his or her own behalf.

An EPA must include statements:

(i) by the Donor, to show that he or she intends the power to continue in spite of any subsequent mental incapacity of his or hers;

(ii)   by the Donor to show that he or she has read or has had read to him or her the information explaining the effect of creating the power; and

(iii)   by the Attorney to show that he or she understands the duty of registration imposed by the Enduring Powers of Attorney Act 1985.

When does the EPA become effective?

The Donor needs to establish when he can rely on the Attorney to handle his or her affairs. The Attorney must be aware of when the power begins and ends so that he or she will meet his or her responsibilities and not exceed the authority. Third parties need to know when they can and should reasonably rely upon and deal with the Attorney.

If there is no indication to the contrary, the EPA will begin immediately after it has been signed by the Donor and the Attorney. However, the Donor may wish to restrict the power by stating that it should not begin until the Donor is incapable of acting on his or her own behalf. The easiest way to establish that condition is by stating in the power that it is not to be used by the Attorney until the need arises to apply for registration.

The Donor can revoke the EPA at any time before it has been registered, as long as he or she is still mentally capable. After the EPA has been registered, it is up to the Court of Protection to cancel registration and revoke the EPA (see page 26).

Highlight

If there is no indication to the contrary, the EPA will begin immediately after it has been signed by the Donor and the Attorney.

EPA: the Donor

2

Granting an EPA allows the Donor to select the person most suitable to protect his or her interests, so a Donor should consider the implications and practicalities of granting such a power. A Donor should be open and communicative with his or her Attorney.

Who may be a Donor and make an EPA?

Any individual who is aged 18 or over, has sufficient mental capacity and is not an undischarged bankrupt can make an EPA. A company or a partnership cannot make an EPA.

Two or more Donors cannot make a joint EPA appointing the same Attorney. Donors must make individual powers and the EPA will not be accepted for registration unless this is complied with.

What does 'sufficient mental capacity' mean?

For the purpose of the Attorney registering an EPA, a Donor's 'mental incapacity' is clearly defined in the Enduring Power of Attorney Act 1985 as being 'incapable by reason of mental disorder of managing and administering [one's own] property and affairs'.

There is, however, no express definition of mental capacity to grant an EPA. To have the mental capacity to be the Donor of an EPA, you must be capable of understanding the nature and effect of the powers granted at the time you made the EPA.

It is not necessary that the Donor be capable of performing all the acts which the EPA authorises, but the Donor cannot authorise the

Attorney to do something which he himself is not legally entitled to do. For example, it is possible that someone suffering from mental illness might be incapable of handling transactions, but capable of understanding the process and consequences of granting an EPA. Similarly, an EPA is valid if a mentally ill person executed it during a period of lucidity. However, if the EPA is made under such circumstances, it would be advisable to obtain medical evidence of the Donor's mental capacity at the time of making the EPA. This could later be needed as evidence of the EPA's validity if there is an objection raised by, for example, one of the Donor's relatives.

What kind of authority can a Donor give in an EPA?

When a Donor makes an EPA, he or she can state what kind of authority the Attorney may have. This can be:

1) A general authority; this means that the Attorney will be able to do anything which the Donor is or was legally able to do.

2) A specific authority; this means that the Donor states the specific acts which he or she has delegated to the Attorney. The Attorney will only have authority for that specific matter.

3) A general or specific authority which has been restricted in some way by the Donor. For example, the Donor does not want the EPA to have immediate effect but wants it to become effective only when he has actually become mentally incapable.

Choosing your Attorney or Attorneys

A Donor may appoint one Attorney or more than one. Careful thought should be given when choosing your Attorney, as they will be dealing closely with your personal affairs. When the Attorney applies to register the EPA (see chapter 5), the Court has the right to refuse to register the power of it considers the Attorney(s) to be unsuitable. Also consider who would be a practical choice of Attorney. Someone

Highlight

Careful thought should be given when choosing your Attorney, as they will be dealing closely with your personal affairs..

living abroad, for example, would not be able to deal with your affairs that easily.

If you appoint more than one Attorney, you must decide how they are to act. They may act either:

1)   'jointly', which means they must all act together and cannot act separately. If one of the joint Attorneys disclaims, dies, becomes bankrupt or mentally incapable, the joint appointment will terminate; or

2)   'jointly and severally', which means they may act together, but also separately if they want to. If one of the Attorneys who has been appointed on a joint and several basis disclaims, dies, becomes bankrupt or mentally incapable, the power will not automatically be terminated as the other(s) can continue to act.

Many Donors appoint family members to be their Attorney(s). For example, they may appoint their spouse as Attorney together with their children, with an informal understanding that the children will not act while the spouse is able to do so.

Restrictions

When a Donor fills in the form to create an EPA, he or she has the opportunity to restrict the extent of the authority which the Attorney has, or to place limitations on dealing with certain parts of the Donor's property. He or she may also choose to appoint different Attorneys to deal with different parts of his or her property. Examples of common restrictions or limitations made by Donors are described overleaf.

Postponing the 'start date' of the EPA

Some Donors do not want the EPA to be effective immediately, but would rather state that it should not come into effect until a time when the Donor has become mentally incapable and the power is registered with the Court of Protection. There are, however, some disadvantages to this stipulation. The Attorney in such circumstances would have no powers until registration of the EPA. This could be extremely inconvenient for all concerned as the registration process takes at least five weeks, if all goes smoothly. If you wanted to include a similar provision, it would be better to state that you do not want the EPA to become effective until the need arises to apply to register the EPA. This will mean that the Attorney would have some limited powers at a useful time, i.e. when the Donor has become mentally incapable, but the EPA has not yet been registered. However, such a restriction would not allow for a situation in which a Donor had a short-term physical or mental incapacity – for example, when unable to write, recovering from an operation.

Restricting the scope of the Attorney's authority

The Donor may want to prevent the Attorney from dealing with a particular part of his or her property or affairs. If you wish to do something similar, you should take care to ensure that you have made other arrangements for the excluded property and that you have not left anything overlooked. Consult a solicitor if you have any doubts.

If the Donor is also a trustee

If as a Donor you are a trustee and your Attorney is a beneficiary of the trust, but you do not want your Attorney to have the power to do anything you can do as a trustee, you should ask a solicitor to help you with your EPA. Bear in mind that co-ownership of a home involves trusteeship; if you do not restrict the EPA, you will delegate power to act in the trust of the jointly owned property to the Attorney if the Attorney is the co-owner. Power to exercise the Donor's trust functions in other circumstances can often be granted for no more than 12 months, but the rules are complicated and if it is important that the Attorney should have this power, legal advice should be taken.

Making gifts

Attorneys are permitted to make some gifts to certain people, including themselves (see pages 11 and 54). Some Donors choose to restrict this power, for example stating that Attorneys should not be able to make gifts to themselves. More radical gifts would in any event require the consent of the Court of Protection if a good case could be made out.

Highlight

If you are a trustee, you can delegate power to ac in the trust by means of your EPA, but only to a beneficiary of the trust, and if you do not want such an Attorney to act i this capacity, you should ask a solicitor to help you with your EPA.

Duties of the Donor

If there are any restrictions on the Donor's power to grant an EPA he or she must specify these to the Attorney, or the Donor will be liable for any damages that result from his or her failure to do so. If, for example, the Attorney breaches a contract with a third party because the Donor did not inform him or her of the existence of that contract, the Donor, not the Attorney, will be liable for any damages sought by the third party.

If any Attorney's actions exceed the limits prescribed in the EPA the Donor is not obliged to validate the Attorney's actions after those actions have taken place – the Attorney acted on his or her own accord. The Donor should, as mentioned above, make certain that the scope of the Attorney's power as indicated in the EPA is made sufficiently clear to prevent such an occasion from arising.

Revoking the EPA

If a Donor changes his or her mind after the EPA has been signed, he or she can revoke the EPA at any time provided he or she is still mentally capable and the EPA has not yet been registered with the Court of Protection. If you want to do so, consult a solicitor who will draft a Deed of Revocation for you.

An EPA cannot be revoked once it has been registered unless and until the Court of Protection confirms the revocation. The Court will require medical evidence that the Donor is mentally capable, or was mentally capable at the time, when he or she revoked the EPA.

EPA: the Attorney

3

Highlight

An Attorney is someone who has been chosen by the Donor to act on his or her behalf in financial matters.

An Attorney is someone who has been chosen by the Donor to act on his or her behalf in financial matters. The Attorney will be able to do anything which the Donor could legally do, such as signing cheques or selling shares.

Who may be an Attorney?

Anyone who is willing, who is over 18 and who is not bankrupt when he or she signs the EPA can be an Attorney. A trust corporation, for example a bank, can also be an Attorney.

Attorneys do not have to live in England or Wales, but if resident abroad they may have difficulty in executing some of the transactions on the Donor's behalf.

Powers and duties of the Attorney

It is important that both the Donor and the Attorney clearly understand the powers and duties of the Attorney. It should be understood that, subject to the exceptions below and any restrictions placed on the power by the Donor, the Attorney can do anything the Donor can legally do. This might include, for example, preparing Tax Returns, making investment decisions, arranging insurance, employing staff or selling property. The Attorney also has the power to make gifts, although the law does limit the scope of this power.

An Attorney may make reasonable gifts (bearing in mind how much money the Donor has) to a charity or to an individual who is related to or connected to the Donor and to himself or herself as Attorney. However, the gifts must be of a seasonal nature, i.e. they must be at Christmas, for birthdays or wedding anniversaries.

What an Attorney cannot do under an EPA

The Attorney cannot:

(i)   execute a Last Will & Testament on behalf of the Donor without the authority of the Court, but the Will-making procedure can take many months and can only be done after registration;

(ii)   take any action concerning the Donor's marriage or divorce;

(iii)   appoint a substitute or successor for him or herself as an Attorney for the Donor;

(iv)   decide questions of health care on behalf of the Donor.

Whether the EPA is general or specific and whether or not it is limited or restricted in any way, its wording must be strictly observed by the Attorney who must not act beyond the authority given by the Donor.

Registration

It is the Attorney's duty to (i) notify the Donor and certain of the Donor's close relatives of his or her intention to register the EPA and to (ii) apply to register the EPA at the Court of Protection when he or she becomes aware that the Donor is, or may soon be, mentally incapable.

Please refer to chapter 5 for detailed instructions concerning the registration procedure.

The Attorney(s) should understand that, after they have notified the Donor and the relatives and applied for registration, they have only limited powers until the EPA is registered. The authority of the Attorney(s) to deal with the Donor's affairs during this time is limited to the maintenance of the Donor and preventing loss to his or her estate.

Standard of care

An Attorney must apply the same standard of care to his duties as an Attorney as he would apply to addressing his own personal concerns. A professional Attorney (for example a solicitor or a bank manager) must carry out the duties as a prudent businessman acting as a trustee would do.

> *Example: When Margaret gave Joe the power to authorise repairs on her car she did not specify how this was to be done. It was Joe's duty to proceed in the most reasonable manner possible, i.e. by using a professional mechanic. When instead Joe sent the car to his 17-year-old neighbour who worked on cars as a weekend hobby, he was not proceeding reasonably or according to convention, and thus could have been liable for damages resulting from poor work on Margaret's car.*

Disclosure of conflict

The Attorney must not undertake acts which conflict with his duties to another person and must disclose any such conflict of interest to the Donor. If he or she is aware that conflicts may arise, it would be better to refuse to act as Attorney in the first place.

Confidentiality

Unless the Donor authorises disclosure, the Attorney must keep the Donor's concerns confidential. He or she may not use his knowledge of the Donor's affairs to his or her own benefit or to the benefit of anyone else.

Accounts

It is advisable for the Attorney to keep complete, up-to-date records of transactions involving the Donor's money, and keep this money apart from his or her own.

Highlight

An Attorney is someone who has been chosen by the Donor to act on his or her behalf in financial matters.

Highlight

It is advisable for the Attorney to keep complete, up-to-date records of transactions involving the Donor's money, and keep this money apart from his or her own.

Compensation for work done as an Attorney

Unless it is expressly specified in the EPA, the Attorney is generally not entitled to compensation, although he or she would be entitled to reimbursement for out-of-pocket expenses. If the Attorney is a professional, he or she may expect compensation and this should be agreed in advance of the appointment.

If your Attorney is also a Trustee for you, the Attorney may not be allowed compensation as Trustees are not allowed to profit from Trusts unless it is expressly authorised by the Trust.

Court of Protection

The Court of Protection can impose additional duties on the Attorney, before registration, as well as after, if it sees indications that the Donor is, or is about to be, mentally incapable. According to the Enduring Power of Attorney Act 1985, the Court has the authority to exercise the following prerogatives:

(i)   to give directions as to the management or disposal by the Attorney of the Donor's property and affairs;

(ii)   to direct the rendering of accounts by the Attorney, and the production of the records he or she keeps for that purpose;

(iii)   to give directions regarding the Attorney's remuneration or expenses, whether or not they are mentioned in the EPA, including the power to make orders to repay excessive remuneration, or to pay additional sums;

(iv)   to require that the Attorney furnish information or produce documents or things which he or she has in his or her possession in his or her capacity as Attorney;

(v)   to give any consent or authority which the Attorney would have had to obtain from a mentally capable Donor;

(vi) to authorise the Attorney to benefit himself, or persons other than the Donor, in some way beyond the general statutory authority.

Disclaiming the role of Attorney

An Attorney may decide that he or she no longer wishes to act as an Attorney. If the Attorney decides to disclaim the power whilst the Donor is still mentally capable (and the power has therefore not been registered), then the Attorney should give notice of his or her disclaimer to the Donor in writing. If the EPA has been registered, the Attorney should give notice in writing to the Court of Protection.

How to prepare an Enduring Power of Attorney

4

You will find in this Law Pack Guide an *Enduring Power of Attorney Form* ready for photocopying and use. This comprises Parts A, B & C. A completed example of the Form has been included on this Guide for guidance, beginning on page 54.

Part A

This gives explanatory notes about filling in the Form. Both the Donor and the Attorney(s) should read the notes carefully before signing the document.

Part B

This is the section of the Form which must be completed by the Donor and it is here that any restrictions on the Power to be granted must be noted. Remember that there can only be one Donor per form.

Part C

This section of the Form must be completed by the Attorney(s).

Completing the Form

You should take care to express clearly in the EPA exactly what you want to authorise. Ambiguous wording can undermine an EPA, either by leading the Court to interpret limitations more narrowly than intended, or allowing an Attorney to exceed the intended limits of the Power.

Example: When Priscilla gave Arthur 'the authority to make an annual gift to an organisation that works with wildlife', she intended that he make such gifts to an organisation that worked to preserve wildlife in its natural habitat. The last thing she wanted was what happened. Arthur misinterpreted her ambiguous wording and made a large contribution to the local zoo. The Court, however, found Arthur's interpretation to be a reasonable one, and the gift was made for each of the following 5 years.

The Court of Protection has the authority to resolve any question on the intent of a limited power. The Courts interpret limited Powers very strictly, so it is important that all wording in the EPA reflects the full intended scope of the Power. After the EPA is registered, the Donor can no longer extend the scope of the Power and can no longer validate acts that the Attorney has taken.

Highlight

The Court of Protection has the authority to resolve any question on the intent of a limited power.

Filling in Part B of the Form as a Donor

The Attorneys

You must name your Attorney(s) and decide whether you want them to act jointly or jointly and severally (see page 7). Remember to delete the statements which do not comply with your wishes.

The Nature of the Authority

You can give your Attorney(s) a general power or a specific power (see page 6 for details). If you want to give a specific power, you need to state what that is in the space provided. Similarly, you will have to decide whether the general or specific Power is in relation to *all* of your property and affairs or only part of them.

In both cases, remember to cross out all the alternatives which do not apply to you.

Restrictions

You may stipulate restrictions on the second page of Part B if you wish. For example, you may want to say that the EPA should not be effective until the need arises to apply for registration.

Registration

You will see that the second page of Part B includes a statement that you (the Donor) intend that the power will continue even if you become mentally incapable. You should understand that this means that your Attorney(s) is under an obligation to apply to register the EPA if he or she believes that you are or are becoming mentally incapable.

Filling in Part C of the Form as an Attorney

If there is more than one Attorney, each of you should fill in a separate Part C.

You will see that the written instructions on the Form state your obligation to apply for registration once the Donor is, or is becoming, mentally incapable. Please see chapter 5 for details on how to do this.

Signing the EPA

If the Donor is mentally capable and understands what the EPA is, he or she should sign the EPA in the presence of a witness, who should then sign their name and add their details in the space provided. The witness should not be one of the Attorneys or the Donor's spouse.

If the Donor is physically unable to sign or is illiterate, then he or she should make a mark and someone, who is not an Attorney or a witness, should sign on the Donor's behalf. A statement should then be put on the form to state that the EPA and explanatory information were read out to the Donor, who appeared to understand it fully. If someone signs on behalf of the Donor, then it should be done in the presence of two witnesses, who should then sign their names and add their details. If you have any doubts, consult a solicitor.

The Attorney(s) must sign the EPA after the Donor and should only sign if he or she believes the Donor has not already become mentally incapable. If there is more than one Attorney, they can sign on different days and with different witnesses at anytime after the Donor has signed the form. Remember that Attorneys must not witness each others signature and a Donor must not witness an Attorney's signature. Please note that a blind person cannot act as a witness.

Registering the EPA

5

It is the Attorney's duty to apply to the Court of Protection to register the EPA when he or she sees evidence that the Donor has become, or is becoming mentally incapable. It is down to the Attorney's judgment as to when this happens. The Attorney may need to take medical advice about whether the Donor is or is not mentally incapable; but no proof is needed of the Donor's mental incapacity to register the power. However, if there is an objection raised to the proposed registration, the Court of Protection will require some medical evidence that the Donor is not mentally capable.

It is in everyone's interests to proceed with the registration as quickly as possible after the Donor has become mentally incapable.

Notification

Before making the application to the Court for the registration of the EPA, the Attorney(s) must give notice of the proposed registration to the Donor and certain close relatives of the Donor. All notices of intention to register the EPA must be made on the prescribed *Form EP1 Notice of intention to apply for registration*. Please see page 60 for completed example.

Notifying the relatives

Notice must be given by the Attorney(s) to at least three relatives of the Donor. Relatives are placed in classes and put in order of priority. If the requirement to give notice to three relatives means that one of a class is notified, then all people in that class must be notified.

Highlight

Notice must be given by the Attorney(s) to at least three relatives of the Donor.

For example:

1) The Donor has a wife, four sons and both parents still alive. The wife and sons would have to be notified.

2) The Donor is a widower with three daughters and two brothers. Only the three daughters would need to receive notification.

If the Donor does not have three living relatives who fall within the prescribed classes, the Attorney(s) should state that on the Application to Register.

Below are the relatives entitled to notice in the order in which they must be notified:

1) The Donor's husband or wife.

2) The Donor's children.

3) The Donor's parents.

4) The Donor's brothers and sisters, whether of the whole or half blood. A person is a relative of the whole blood to another if they share two common parents. A relative who shares only one common parent is a relative of the half blood.

5) The widow or widower of a child of the Donor.

6) The Donor's grandchildren.

7) The children of the Donor's brothers and sisters of the whole blood.

8) The children of the Donor's brothers and sisters of the half blood.

9) The Donor's uncles and aunts of the whole blood.

10) The children of the Donor's uncles and aunts of the whole blood.

A person is not entitled to notice if:

• his or her name or address is unknown to the Attorney

• he or she is less than 18 years of age

- he or she is mentally incapable

Notification of the relatives may be done by first-class post. It does not need to be done in person.

What if one or more of the Attorneys are also notifiable relatives?

This will often be the case, as many Donors choose to have their spouse or children as their Attorney(s). If an Attorney is also a notifiable relative, then they can count themselves as having been notified and there is no need to fill in *Form EP1*. For example, if the Attorney is one of the Donor's three children and the Donor has no spouse, then only the two children who are not Attorneys need to be notified.

Notifying the Donor

The Attorney must give notice to the Donor in person by actually handing it to the Donor, even if the Donor appears not to realise what is happening. Notification to the Donor cannot be done by post.

Is it always necessary to give notice to the Donor and/to the relatives?

The law does allow exemptions from the requirement to give notice in exceptional circumstances, as many Attorneys find it distressing to have to inform Donors of their failing mental capacity. Application for dispensation from the requirement to serve notice on anyone entitled to receive it, including the Donor, can be made to the Public Trustee on *Form EP3 General form of application* included in this Guide and the original EPA should also be sent.

However, the Public Trustee is unlikely to give a dispensation unless the circumstances are truly exceptional as it is the Donor's right to be informed and to be able to object to the proposed registration. Dispensation will normally only be given where it can be shown that the Donor would be unduly harmed or distressed by the news.

Who should give the notices if there is more than one Attorney?

Attorneys appointed jointly must give notices jointly or they will not be deemed to be valid. If there is more than one Attorney appointed to act jointly and severally, then they should give the notices jointly if they both want to act following the registration of the power. If only one of them gives the notices, then the other(s) must also be sent *Form EP1*. If the notices of intention to register do not name all of the Attorneys, then registration will take place but will be limited to only those Attorneys whose names were on the *Form EP1*.

Application

Who must apply?

If Attorneys have been appointed to act jointly, they must all apply for registration in order for the power to be valid. This is necessary because under a joint power the Attorneys cannot act without each other. If Attorneys have been appointed to act jointly and severally, they do not all have to apply but only those who do will continue to have power.

In some cases more than one EPA may have been granted by one donor. In these cases each EPA must be registered separately.

The application form

The application to register the EPA must be sent to the Public Trust Office on *Form EP2 Application for registration*. It is not acceptable to apply by letter. The completed Form must be accompanied by the original EPA and a cheque for the registration fee (currently £75), made payable to 'The Public Trust Office'.

What if there is financial hardship?

Normally, no application will be considered if the registration fee has not been paid. However, it may be that the Attorney(s) is experiencing financial difficulties and cannot afford to pay the fee straightaway. If this is the case, the Attorney(s) should state this in a covering letter with the *Application*. The Public Trustee may allow the application to proceed in cases of genuine financial hardship, as long as payment is made as soon as money can be obtained from the Donor's funds.

Highlight

If Attorneys have been appointed to act jointly, they must all apply for registration in order for the power to be valid.

When must the Application be made?

It must be made by first-class post within 10 days of the day on which the last of the notices to the Donor and the relatives was given. Send the *Application* to:

> The Public Trust Office Protection Division
> Stewart House
> 24 Kingsway
> London WC2B 6JX

Objections to the registration of the EPA

The Public Trust Office will not register the EPA immediately upon receipt of it. They will check through the papers and wait for a period of five weeks from the date of the last notification on a *Form EP1* before registering. Registration will only take place after this time if no objections have been received during the five-week period.

Grounds on which objections may be raised

The grounds for objection are listed on the *Notice of intention to apply for registration* (*Form EP1*, page 61). Any objection which is not related to one of the five grounds will not be investigated by the Public Trustee. For example, relatives have no automatic right to be named as Attorney and cannot object that they are not one of the Attorneys named on the EPA.

A person wishing to object to the registration of a power must submit to the Court of Protection in writing his or her name and address, the Donor's name and address, the objector's relationship to the Donor, the Attorney's name and address, and the grounds of the objection. A copy of the objection may be supplied to the Attorney by the Public Trust Office and, if the disagreement cannot be sorted out between the Attorney and the objector, the Court of Protection may fix a date for a hearing. If the objection is upheld, the EPA will be cancelled and will not be registered. Otherwise, the EPA will be returned to the Attorney, stamped and sealed by the Court of Protection, and thus registered.

Highlight

The application must be made by first-class post within 10 days of the day on which the last of the notices to the Donor and the relatives was given.

Cancellation of registration

Once the registration is complete, the Court will treat any objection as an application to cancel the registration. The Court may direct that an application to cancel registration be made on *Form EP3*. The Court can cancel a registration for the following reasons:

1) If it confirms the revocation of the power by the Donor, which must have been made when he was mentally capable, or receives notice of disclaimer by the Attorney.

2) If it gives a direction revoking the power upon exercising any of its powers under part VII of the Mental Health Act 1983.

3) If it is satisfied that the Donor is, and is likely to remain, mentally capable.

4) If it is satisfied that the power has expired or has been revoked by the death or bankruptcy of the Donor, the death, mental incapacity or bankruptcy of the Attorney or, if the Attorney is a corporation, upon its winding up or dissolution.

5) If it is satisfied that the power was not a valid and continuing enduring power when the registration was effected.

6) If it is satisfied that fraud or undue pressure was used to induce the Donor to create the power.

7) If it is satisfied that the Attorney's relationship to or connection with the Donor makes him or her unsuitable to be the Donor's Attorney.

The Court should always be notified of the death or recovery of the Donor.

Highlight

The Court may, on its own, exercise the powers under the EPA if it has reason to believe that the Donor is mentally incapable and that action on behalf of the Donor is necessary to protect the Donor.

Summary of the registration process

1) The Attorney(s) believe(s) that the Donor is, or is becoming, mentally incapable.

2) The Attorney(s) give(s) notice on *Form EP1* to at least three relatives in order of priority (see page 22) and the

Donor in person, of their intention to register the EPA. All notices must be served within 14 days of each other.

3) Within 10 days of the date on which the last notice to the Donor or to relatives was given, the Attorney(s) must send the *Application for registration Form EP2*, together with the original *EPA* and the registration fee.

4) The Public Trust Office will inspect the paperwork and hold it for a period of 5 weeks from the date on which the last notice on a *Form EP1* was served. During this period, anyone may object to the registration.

5) If no objections are received and all the papers are in order, the EPA will be registered after the expiry of the 5-week period.

6) If objections are received, they will be investigated, following which the EPA will either be revoked or cancelled or it will be registered.

Where can I get more information about registering EPAs?

Further enquiries about registering an EPA only may be made by post or in person at:

The Enquiries Branch
The Public Trust Office Protection Division
Stewart House
24 Kingsway
London WC2B 6JX
Telephone 020 7664 7000

Highlight

The Public Trust Office carries out administrative functions on behalf of the Court of Protection and does not give advice on actually making the Enduring Power of Attorney.

The Public Trust Office carries out administrative functions on behalf of the Court of Protection and does *not* give advice on actually making the Enduring Power of Attorney. You should consult a solicitor or Citizens Advice Bureau if you have questions about your legal rights and obligations, or need further assistance in preparing these forms.

General Powers of Attorney

A General Power of Attorney is, like an EPA, a statutory form for authorising an Attorney to act on the Donor's behalf and in his or her name. But the important difference between an EPA and a General Power is that a General Power is automatically annulled in the event of the Donor becoming mentally incapable, whereas an EPA remains in force, subject to its registration. A General Power is a straightforward authorisation, without the added complications of an EPA; as such it is a straightforward form to fill out (see completed example on page 69).

Highlight

Unlike an EPA there is no provision for limiting the scope of the Power; but otherwise the extent and scope of the two kinds of power of attorney are the same.

A General Power is a useful means of creating a power of attorney for a specific period or event, when the age and health of the Donor make it unlikely that he or she could become mentally incapable during the duration of the power. The need for a General Power might arise, for example, when a person goes abroad for some time and wishes to entrust the management of business interests to a family member.

The rules governing who can be a Donor or an Attorney are the same as for an EPA, i.e. they must over 18, of full mental capacity and not an undischarged bankrupt.

Scope and restrictions

Once a General Power is granted the Attorney has full legal authority to take decisions and actions on the Donor's behalf, as if the Donor were taking them himself, except that the Attorney cannot make gifts even to the limited extent which an EPA allows. Unlike an EPA there is no provision for limiting the scope of the power in a General Power;

but otherwise the extent and scope of the two are the same. This could be signing letters and cheques, or buying and selling property and shares, unless held in trust. A General Power is very wide-ranging and gives an Attorney a great deal of power (it *is* possible to give a limited power of attorney in a different form, but this is beyond the scope of this Guide and further information should be obtained from a solicitor). In effect, an Attorney can do anything he or she thinks fit. However, the Power does not cover functions of the Donor which relate to certain special personal responsibilities. For example, an Attorney cannot normally perform in the Donor's role as a trustee and cannot perform in the Donor's role as personal representative (i.e. administrator) of someone's estate. With regard to delegation of trustee functions, see page 6. An Attorney cannot execute the Donor's Last Will & Testament, take action concerning the Donor's marriage or delegate his or her Power.

It is important to bear in mind that the Donor does remain liable for the actions of the Attorney. Clearly, the extent of the Power is such that it should only be given to somebody the Donor trusts implicitly.

Highlight

Unlike an EPA there is no provision for limiting the scope of the power in a General Power; but otherwise the extent and scope of the two are the same.

Duration

If the Donor becomes mentally incapable the GPA is automatically annulled. Otherwise, a General Power remains valid until it is revoked. Powers can be revoked orally, but to avoid misunderstanding it is wise to write 'cancelled' on the original form or simply tear it up.

The General Power would also be revoked by the death or bankruptcy of the Donor or Attorney.

Completing your General Power

First, take a copy of the form included in this Guide. Also refer to the completed example on page 69.

You should insert the date on which the Power is to begin. This should be the same as the date it is signed.

The Donor should enter his or her full name and address. Only one Donor may make a GPA.

Enter the full name and address of the Attorney or Attorneys. As with an EPA, if you are appointing more than one Attorney they may be appointed 'jointly' or 'jointly and severally'. There is an explanation of these terms on page 7. Once you have decided how they are to act, delete as appropriate.

The Donor should sign the General Power in the presence of a witness who should also sign it. An Attorney cannot act as a witness. Once this is done the General Power is in force, until revoked.

What is a Living Will?

A Living Will is an advance declaration of your wishes on medical treatments which you could be given in the future. Treatment could be for any illness you have now or which you develop, or for ill health as a result of any accident which you might suffer. It is a way of letting your doctors and family know what medical procedures you would not want to receive if, at a time the treatment could be given to you, you are unable to communicate your wishes to them yourself because of mental and/or physical incapacity.

It is important to realise that you can only use a Living Will to *refuse* certain treatments or procedures. It is not possible to request specific treatments or procedures. You can use your Living Will to say what quality of life and level of treatment you would consider acceptable if you became incapacitated by a terminal disease or if you were in a persistent vegetative state (an irreversible coma where you are only kept alive by artificial feeding mechanisms).

The Living Will can be a general statement of your wishes and/or it can direct your doctors and family on your wishes in relation to specific illnesses and their possible treatments. You can also appoint someone you trust — maybe a close friend or family member – with whom you would like doctors to consult about any medical procedures which could be administered to you. This person, who is referred to as a Health Care Proxy, would be aware of your views and would be able to communicate your wishes to medical staff.

This Guide includes a Form for writing your Living Will, appointing a Health Care Proxy if you wish.

Highlight

The Living Will can be a general statement of your wishes and/or it can direct your doctors and family on your wishes in relation to specific illnesses and their possible treatments.

The difference between a Living Will and an ordinary Will

A Living Will is only concerned with medical treatment when you are still alive. You cannot use it to communicate your wishes on any matters normally dealt with by an ordinary Will, or Last Will & Testament. In other words you cannot use it to determine who will inherit your property when you die, who will be your executors, or who will be guardians to your children. If you need an ordinary Will, we recommend the *Law Pack Last Will and Testament Guide*, available from bookshops and stationers.

The difference between a Living Will and an Enduring Power of Attorney

When you make an Enduring Power of Attorney, you can give your Attorney a general or limited power to conduct business, legal and financial transactions on your behalf. However, an Attorney is not permitted to make any decisions on health care matters. You therefore need to make a Living Will and appoint a Health Care Proxy if you want to delegate decisions on your future health care.

Are Living Wills valid and enforceable?

At present, there are no laws in England and Wales about Living Wills, although a Draft Bill to make Living Wills legal, written by the Law Commission, is being considered by Parliament. The extent to which a Living Will will be considered enforceable at the moment depends on the way it is written and what it asks or directs doctors to do.

Advance directives

An informed and competent adult has the right to refuse medical procedures if he or she wants, unless the refusal harms others or conflicts with any law either at the time or in advance, except where there is a risk of contagion or if it is a matter of hygiene or comfort. This is what is known as an 'advance directive'. The British Medical Association supports the use of advance directives and says that 'an

Highlight

In law, an informed and competent adult has the right to refuse medical procedures if he or she wants, unless the refusal harms others or conflicts with any law unambiguous and informed advance refusal is as valid as a contemporaneous decision'. Recent cases have supported the view that an advance refusal of treatment will be valid and enforceable if the following are complied with:

- you were mentally capable of making the decision to refuse medical treatment;

- you understood what the consequences of the refusal would be;

- the situation that has arisen is clearly of the type to which your refusal was meant to apply;

- the decision was your own and was not made under the influence of any other person.

Remember, the advance directives to which a Living Will gives effect only apply to refusals of certain treatments. An adult cannot demand that certain procedures are given to him or her and, similarly, cannot say in advance what should be given. A Living Will which states that certain procedures should be administered – for example, that a lethal injection should be given in the final stages of a terminal illness – will not be valid and enforceable.

Is there anything which cannot be refused in advance?

Yes, generally, you cannot refuse the essentials of good medical and nursing practice. This will include, for instance, basic hygiene measures. It will also extend to pain relief and management of distressing symptoms, such as vomiting. You can refuse in advance to be given food and drink in certain circumstances and you can refuse tube feeding. However, the British Medical Association Code on Advance Directives makes it clear that food and drink should be available for patients and offered to them (though not forced on them) at all times.

Advance statements

You can make advance statements of your wishes on certain treatments under the section 'Additional Directions on Future Health Care' on the Living Will Form (see page 71). An Advance Statement differs from an Advance Directive in that doctors are not obliged to follow your wishes as expressed in a Statement, but they are obliged to observe your wishes in an Advance Directive. This is because Advance Directives deal with refusals of treatment and only categorical refusals of treatments will be binding. For example, you may want to state that you would not want to receive electric shock treatment: doctors will take account of this and will treat this directive with respect. However, if you state that you would want to receive a particular treatment for cancer (rather than refuse something), then your request would not be binding although it may have persuasive force on doctors.

Health Care Proxies

It is unlikely that a Health Care Proxy's decisions would have legal force. However, it is recognised that it is helpful for patients to nominate Proxies to express their wishes as it adds support to an advance statement or if an advance directive cannot be found in time.

Living Wills and euthanasia

An advance directive in a Living Will is not the same as euthanasia. Euthanasia and assisted suicides are not legal and you cannot write a Living Will directing doctors and relatives to act in this way. Anyone who helps you die or kill yourself is committing a criminal offence.

What are the benefits of making a Living Will?

Many people are concerned about what will happen to them if they become very ill and are unable to communicate their wishes to anyone. Many fear the loss of dignity and the significantly decreased quality of life which can result from degenerative health conditions. Medical technology has now advanced to such a degree that people can be kept alive even when they are brain dead.

Some people, after careful consideration and discussion with their doctors, decide that they do not want to receive treatments which would result in a meaningless and prolonged artificial existence. They to have the benefit of recording their decisions and the peace of mind of knowing this will be communicated to the doctors. Opinions on how long a life can and should be prolonged have become increasingly subjective and it is increasingly acknowledged that people should be allowed to have a say in their future medical care.

Example: John has been lying in a nursing home bed for two and a half years. There is no evidence that he can hear, see, think or feel. John's breathing is controlled by a ventilator connected by a tracheotomy tube implanted in his throat. His nourishment and wastes are controlled by more tubes. His friends and family feel certain that he would not want to live this way, but, technically, John is alive.

If you go into a hospital or a nursing home without specific written instructions, or appropriate notes of conversations with doctors having been made on your medical notes, the institution you enter will be legally bound to keep you alive by whatever means are deemed necessary and appropriate by the medical staff. With a Living Will, you express your rational views on the circumstances in which you would not want such attempts to keep you alive to continue. A Living Will which has been made when a patient is in good health is advantageous later on as it is good evidence of your true feelings.

Doctors are sometimes reluctant to honour the refusals by seriously ill patients because they cannot be certain the decision is rationally made. Another advantage of a Living Will is that you can let your family know what you want. Many families do not want to accept that their loved one is not going to recover and therefore feel that they have to try any procedure which is available.

Remember that you can change your mind at any time about a prior written directive in a Living Will and consent to treatment which you had previously decided to refuse.

What else should I think about?

You should bear in mind that your views may change over time. You views may also change if/when you become ill. You must remember that you can alter your directions at any stage if you want. Advances in medical treatments may also cause you to change your mind.

Should I discuss my Living Will with others?

You are not bound to consult anyone when drawing up your Living Will. However, a Living Will involves other people in carrying out the decisions you have made. It is therefore strongly advised that you do discuss your wishes with those close to you and with medical staff who treat you.

Your family

Your spouse, immediate family and perhaps religious adviser will be more likely to support your decision if you have fully discussed the issues with them in advance.

Your doctors

It is extremely important that you discuss your views with your doctor(s), not only when you make your Living Will but at regular intervals after you have done so, too. Your doctor(s) will be able to advise you on any new techniques or treatments which might become available and which might make you change your mind on certain statements made in your Living Will. Your doctor will want to make sure you are fully aware of the medical options available to you and that your Living Will expresses your true wishes. You will also want to be certain that your doctor will honour your requests and your Living Will should be included in your medical records. Some doctors have moral or ethical objections to Living Wills. It is very important that there is discussion so that your doctor can inform you of his or her views and make other doctors aware of yours. You may wish to change your doctor if this happens.

Highlight

It is extremely important that you discuss your views with your doctor(s), not only when you make your Living Will but at regular intervals after you have done so, too.

Your Health Care Proxy

The individual who will act for you as your Proxy should fully understand your wishes so he or she can make decisions which most closely coincide with the decisions you would have made had you been capable. This may become very important if you make a Living Will which, for example, does not mention a specific illness or situation which later affects you. If they are fully aware of how you would have viewed it, they can then give invaluable advice to the doctor(s).

Preparing a Living Will

8

As there are no laws governing Living Wills, there are no specific eligibility requirements. It is assumed that anyone who is 18 or older and who is mentally competent can prepare a Living Will. Being mentally competent in this context means that you understand what you are proposing in your Living Will, you can consider it and come to a rational decision and understand the effect that your decisions will have.

Highlight

The British Medical Association recognises that children are also entitled to have their iews taken into account, ut their views will not be gally binding on doctors.

The British Medical Association recognises that children are also entitled to have their views taken into account, but their views will not be legally binding on doctors.

The form of your Living Will should be in writing and should be signed by you. Your signature should be witnessed. If you want to record a Living Will on cassette or video, do so only in addition to providing a clear written version.

What are my options and how are my wishes expressed in a Living Will?

This Guide allows you to make your wishes known. The *Living Will Form* (see page 70), has some general directives and statements about future health care and what you consider to be an acceptable quality of life. It is impossible to anticipate every consideration which might later become relevant to your future health care or to know what medical treatments might be necessary, effective or likely to be administered. However, if you wish to add certain specific directions

– perhaps about existing health care conditions or forms of treatment – then there is space for you to do so.

Pregnancy

If you are a woman and it is possible that you might become pregnant at some point in the future, you should consider how you would feel about the directions or requests you have made in your Living Will if you were pregnant. It is likely that your Living Will will not be considered to be valid if you are pregnant, unless you leave specific instructions, as medical procedures may be administered to try and help the foetus.

How are Living Wills witnessed?

Your Living Will should be witnessed by a mentally competent adult. Your witness should not be someone who might be a beneficiary under your ordinary Will, or the spouse of a beneficiary.

Where should Living Wills be kept?

It is important that people are aware that you have a Living Will, as, if your family and doctors do not know of its existence, or are not sure if it still exists, then medical procedures could be administered to you in good faith which you would not have wanted.

It is a good idea to have several copies of the signed and witnessed Living Will and leave them with your spouse, your family, perhaps a good friend and with your doctor and/or hospital notes. Some people decide to have a card in their wallet alerting anyone who may attend to them in an accident of the existence of a Living Will and where it may be found.

Revising a Living Will

It is important that you consider the terms of your Living Will at regular intervals so that you can be aware of the latest position and others can be aware that your views are current. You may like to add your signature and the date to the bottom of your Living Will when you have done so. There is no need to make a new Living Will every time. However, if you want to make any changes to your Living Will, you should re-do it. If there is a Living Will which has some amendments it may well look like you were not sure, or that it has been tampered with and so will not be valid. The *Living Will Form* in this Guide has space at the end for you to show that you have reconsidered it and your views still stand.

Revoking your Living Will

You always have the right to revoke your Living Will. The easiest way of doing this is by tearing it up or writing "revoked" or "cancelled" on it clearly. Remember that, if you have made several copies of your Living Will and distributed them to various people, you should tear up those copies too and inform the individuals concerned in the change in your opinions.

A later Living Will will automatically revoke an earlier one. However, it is better not to rely on this so as to avoid confusion amongst your family and doctors.

Instructions for completing your Living Will

You should first take a photocopy of the blank *Living Will Form* appearing on pages 70 and 71. Then refer to the completed example of a Living Will on page 72.

Personal details

You should fill in your name, address, date of birth, National Health Number and your doctor's details in the first section. Write clearly in dark ink or type the details.

Medical treatment you wish to refuse

This section allows you to make advance directives to refuse future medical treatments which would prolong your life or keep you alive by artificial means. You should read this Guide carefully and consult with your doctors before you fill in this section.

If, after consideration, you agree with the statements, you should put a tick in the boxes after the statements on the right hand side. If you do not agree with the statements, you should cross the statement out entirely to avoid confusion amongst your relatives and doctors.

You will see that there are a number of blank spaces which you need to fill in. For example, you might want two independent medical practitioners' opinions on your health and chances of recovery.

Medical treatment you wish to accept

If you want to accept treatment to manage pain or relieve distressing symptoms, then put a tick in the box after the statement. Otherwise, cross out the entire paragraph. Bear in mind that your doctors will be obliged to provide some degree of basic medical care anyway.

If you may become pregnant

You should consider what you would want to happen if you were pregnant. It is important to discuss this with your doctor if you are unsure. If you would not normally want to receive medical interventions, but would be prepared to accept them if you were pregnant, then you should tick the box at the end of the statement. Bear in mind that medical treatments may be administered to you anyway if the courts say so, in order to protect your unborn child.

Health Care Proxy

You should fill in the name and address of anybody you wish to appoint as your Proxy. Make sure you have discussed it fully with him or her first and they are willing to be named.

Additional directions on health care ━━

You will see that there is a space for you to fill in any additional directions or wishes you may have. For example, you may already be suffering from a particular illness and have strong views about particular treatments which you can envisage being administered to you in the future. Some people may wish to request that a particular person, perhaps a family member or friend, be contacted to come to be with them if their death is imminent. You may wish to receive treatments temporarily to keep you alive until they arrive, if this is possible. You need to consider your options carefully.

Signatures

Once you have completed your *Living Will Form* and you are happy with what it says and the effects it will have, you should sign the Form and add the date. You should sign in the presence of a witness, who should also sign and date the Form (see page 40).

After you and the witness have signed the Form, you should make copies of it and store it with the appropriate people.

Highlight

Once you have completed your Living W Form and you are happy with what is says and th effects it will have, you should sign the Form an add the date.

Affirming your Living Will

At the end of the Form is a space for signing the Living Will at some future date to show that you still have the same beliefs as set out in your Living Will. Remember to sign the Form in the presence of a witness as above and add the date when you do so.

Glossary of useful terms

A–G

Advance Directives – a written record of decisions about your future health care, given effect by a Living Will.

Attorney – a person who has authority to act on behalf of another.

Capacity – competence to enter into a legally binding agreement.

Court of Protection – a court that administers the property and affairs of persons of unsound mind.

Delegate – to grant authority to a person to act on behalf of another person.

Disclaim – to refuse or renounce a right or authority.

Donor – a person who grants a power of attorney.

Enduring Power of Attorney – a power of attorney that remains in effect during the incapacity of the grantor.

Euthanasia – literally 'a good death', refers to the practice of taking active measures to end the suffering of a terminally ill patient.

Execute – to sign or otherwise complete the formalities of a legal document.

General Power of Attorney – a power of attorney that is automatically annulled after the Donor becomes mentally incapable.

H–T

Health Care Proxy – An individual appointed in a Living Will whom doctors may consult on a patient's health care.

Limited power – an authority that is restricted to specified acts or type of acts, or to a specified time period.

Ratification – confirmation of an act or of the validity of an act.

Registration – the process through which an enduring power of attorney is placed under the jurisdiction of the Court of Protection.

Resuscitate – to revive or bring back to consciousness.

Revoke – to take back, withdraw or cancel.

Statute – an Act of Parliament.

Testamentary Will – a legal document that sets out the wishes of the Testator for the distribution of his or her estate and certain other matters after his or her death.

Trust – an arrangement under which a person or persons (the trustee or trustees) hold and manage property for the benefit of another person or persons (the trust beneficiary or beneficiaries).

The forms in this Guide

ENDURING POWER OF ATTORNEY

Part A: About using this form

1. **You may choose one attorney or more than one.** If you choose one attorney then you must delete everything between the square brackets on the first page of the form. If you choose more than one, you must decide whether they are able to act:
   - Jointly (that is, they must all act together and cannot act separately) or
   - Jointly and severally (that is, they can all act together but they can also act separately if they wish).

   On the first page of the form, show what you have decided by crossing out one of the alternatives.

2. **If you give your attorney(s) general power** in relation to all your property and affairs, it means that they will be able to deal with your money or property and may be able to sell your house.

3. **If you don't want your attorney(s) to have such wide powers**, you can include any restrictions you like. For example, you can include a restriction that your attorney(s) must not act on your behalf until they have reason to believe that you are becoming mentally incapable; or a restriction as to what your attorney(s) may do. Any restrictions you choose must be written or typed where indicated on the second page of the form.

4. **If you are a trustee** (and please remember that co-ownership of a home involves trusteeship), you should seek legal advice if you want your attorney(s) to act as a trustee on your behalf.

5. **Unless you put in a restriction preventing it** your attorney(s) will be able to use any of your money or property to make any provision which you yourself might be expected to make for their own needs or the needs of other people. Your attorney(s) will also be able to use your money to make gifts, but only for reasonable amounts in relation to the value of your money and property.

6. **Your attorney(s) can recover the out-of-pocket expenses** of acting as your attorney(s). If your attorney(s) are professional people, for example solicitors or accountants, they may be able to charge for their professional services as well. You may wish to provide expressly for remuneration of your attorney(s) (although if they are trustees they may not be allowed to accept it).

7. **If your attorney(s) have reason to believe** that you have become or are becoming mentally incapable of managing your affairs, your attorney(s) will have to apply to the Court of Protection for registration of this power.

8. **Before applying to the Court of Protection for registration** of this power, your attorney(s) must give written notice that that is what they are going to do, to you and your nearest relatives as defined in the Enduring Powers of Attorney Act 1985. You or your relatives will be able to object if you or they disagree with registration.

9. **This is a simplified explanation** of what the Enduring Powers of Attorney Act 1985 and the Rules and Regulations say. If you need more guidance, you or your advisers will need to look at the Act itself and the Rules and Regulations. The Rules are the Court of Protection (Enduring Powers of Attorney) Rules 1986 (Statutory Instrument 1986 No. 127). The Regulations are the Enduring Powers of Attorney (Prescribed Form) Regulations 1990 (Statutory Instrument 1990 No. 1376).

10. **Note to Attorney(s)**
    After the power has been registered you should notify the Court of Protection if the donor dies or recovers.

11. **Note to Donor**
    Some of these explanatory motes may not apply to the form you are using if it has already been adapted to suit your particular requirements.

YOU CAN CANCEL THIS POWER AT ANY TIME BEFORE IT HAS TO BE REGISTERED

Part B: To be completed by the 'donor' (the person appointing the attorney(s))

Don't sign this form unless you understand what it means

Please read the notes in the margin which follow and which are part of the form itself.
Donor's name and address.

Donor's date of birth.

See note 1 on the front of this form. If you are appointing only one attorney you should cross out everything between the square brackets. If appointing more than two attorneys please give the additional name(s) on an attached sheet.

Cross out the one which does not apply (see note 1 on the front of this form).

Cross out the one which does not apply (see note 2 on the front of this form). Add any additional powers.

If you don't want the attorney(s) to have general power, you must give details here of what authority you are giving the attorney(s).

Cross out the one which does not apply.

I _____

of _____

born on _____

appoint _____

of _____

● [and _____

of _____

● jointly
● jointly and severally]
to be my attorney(s) for the purpose of the Enduring Powers of Attorney Act 1985
● with general authority to act on my behalf
● with authority to do the following on my behalf:

in relation to

● all my property and affairs
● the following property and affairs:

Part B: continued

Please read the notes in the margin which follow and which are part of the form itself.
If there are restrictions or conditions, insert them here; if not, cross out these words if you wish (see note 3 on the front of this form).

● subject to the following restrictions and conditions:

I intend that this power shall continue even if I become mentally incapable.

I have read or have had read to me the notes in Part A which are part of, and explain, this form.

If this form is being signed at your direction: —
● the person signing must not be an attorney or any witness (to Parts B or C);
● you must add a statement that this form has been signed at your direction;
● a second witness is necessary (please see below).

Your signature (or mark).

Signed by me as a deed _____
and delivered

Date.

on _____

Someone must witness your signature.

Signature of witness.

in the presence of _____

Your attorney(s) cannot be your witness. It is not advisable for your husband or wife to be your witness.

Full name of witness _____

Address of witness _____

_____

_____

A second witness is only necessary if this form is not being signed by you personally but at your direction (for example, if a physical disability prevents you from signing).

Signature of second witness.

in the presence of _____

Full name of witness _____

Address of witness _____

_____

_____

Part C: To be completed by the attorney(s)

Note 1. This form may be adapted to provide for execution by a corporation.
2. If there is more than one attorney additional sheets in the form as shown below must be added to this Part C.

Please read the notes in the margin which follow and which are part of the form itself.

Don't sign this form before the donor has signed Part B or if, in your opinion, the donor was already mentally incapable at the time of signing Part B.

If this form is being signed at your direction: —

- the person signing must not be an attorney or any witness (to Parts B or C);
- you must add a statement that this form has been signed at your direction;
- a second witness is necessary (please see below).

Signature (or mark) of attorney.

Date.

Signature of witness.

The attorney must sign the form and his signature must be witnessed. The donor may not be the witness and one attorney may not witness the signature of the other.

A second witness is only necessary if this form is not being signed by you personally but at your direction (for example, if a physical disability prevents you from signing).
Signature of second witness.

I understand that I have a duty to apply to the Court for the registration of this form under the Enduring Powers of Attorney Act 1985 when the donor is becoming or has become mentally incapable.

I also understand my limited power to use the donor's property to benefit persons other than the donor.

I am not a minor

Signed by me as a deed _____
and delivered

on _____

in the presence of _____

Full name of witness _____

Address of witness _____

_____

_____

---

in the presence of _____

Full name of witness _____

Address of witness _____

_____

_____

Completed example of Enduring Power of Attorney

ENDURING POWER OF ATTORNEY

Part A: About using this form

1. **You may choose one attorney or more than one.** If you choose one attorney then you must delete everything between the square brackets on the first page of the form. If you choose more than one, you must decide whether they are able to act:
   - Jointly (that is, they must all act together and cannot act separately) or
   - Jointly and severally (that is, they can all act together but they can also act separately if they wish).
   On the first page of the form, show what you have decided by crossing out one of the alternatives.

2. **If you give your attorney(s) general power** in relation to all your property and affairs, it means that they will be able to deal with your money or property and may be able to sell your house.

3. **If you don't want your attorney(s) to have such wide powers,** you can include any restrictions you like. For example, you can include a restriction that your attorney(s) must not act on your behalf until they have reason to believe that you are becoming mentally incapable; or a restriction as to what your attorney(s) may do. Any restrictions you choose must be written or typed where indicated on the second page of the form.

4. **If you are a trustee** (and please remember that co-ownership of a home involves trusteeship), you should seek legal advice if you want your attorney(s) to act as a trustee on your behalf.

5. **Unless you put in a restriction preventing it** your attorney(s) will be able to use any of your money or property to make any provision which you yourself might be expected to make for their own needs or the needs of other people. Your attorney(s) will also be able to use your money to make gifts, but only for reasonable amounts in relation to the value of your money and property.

6. **Your attorney(s) can recover the out-of-pocket expenses** of acting as your attorney(s). If your attorney(s) are professional people, for example solicitors or accountants, they may be able to charge for their professional services as well. You may wish to provide expressly for remuneration of your attorney(s) (although if they are trustees they may not be allowed to accept it).

7. **If your attorney(s) have reason to believe** that you have become or are becoming mentally incapable of managing your affairs, your attorney(s) will have to apply to the Court of Protection for registration of this power.

8. **Before applying to the Court of Protection for registration** of this power, your attorney(s) must give written notice that that is what they are going to do, to you and your nearest relatives as defined in the Enduring Powers of Attorney Act 1985. You or your relatives will be able to object if you or they disagree with registration.

9. **This is a simplified explanation** of what the Enduring Powers of Attorney Act 1985 and the Rules and Regulations say. If you need more guidance, you or your advisers will need to look at the Act itself and the Rules and Regulations. The Rules are the Court of Protection (Enduring Powers of Attorney) Rules 1986 (Statutory Instrument 1986 No. 127). The Regulations are the Enduring Powers of Attorney (Prescribed Form) Regulations 1990 (Statutory Instrument 1990 No. 1376).

10. **Note to Attorney(s)** After the power has been registered you should notify the Court of Protection if the donor dies or recovers.

11. **Note to Donor** Some of these explanatory notes may not apply to the form you are using if it has already been adapted to suit your particular requirements.

YOU CAN CANCEL THIS POWER AT ANY TIME BEFORE IT HAS TO BE REGISTERED

(Continued on next page)

Completed example of Enduring Power of Attorney (continued)

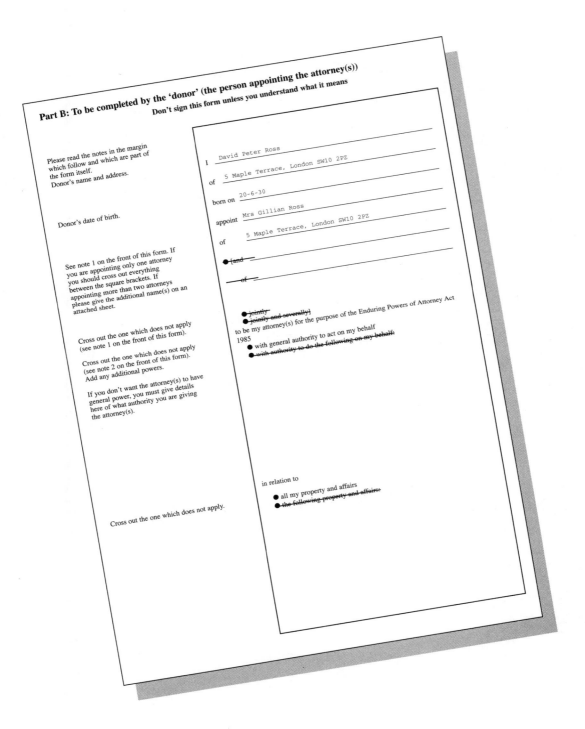

Part B: To be completed by the 'donor' (the person appointing the attorney(s))

Don't sign this form unless you understand what it means

Please read the notes in the margin which follow and which are part of the form itself.
Donor's name and address.

Donor's date of birth.

See note 1 on the front of this form. If you are appointing only one attorney you should cross out everything between the square brackets. If appointing more than two attorneys please give the additional name(s) on an attached sheet.

Cross out the one which does not apply (see note 1 on the front of this form).

Cross out the one which does not apply (see note 2 on the front of this form). Add any additional powers.

If you don't want the attorney(s) to have general power, you must give details here of what authority you are giving the attorney(s).

Cross out the one which does not apply.

I   David Peter Ross

of   5 Maple Terrace, London SW10 2PZ

born on   20-6-30

appoint   Mrs Gillian Ross

of   5 Maple Terrace, London SW10 2PZ

● [and

● of

● jointly

● jointly and severally]

to be my attorney(s) for the purpose of the Enduring Powers of Attorney Act 1985

● with general authority to act on my behalf

● with authority to do the following on my behalf

in relation to

● all my property and affairs

● the following property and affairs:

(Continued on next page)

Completed example of Enduring Power of Attorney (continued)

Part B: continued

Please read the notes in the margin which follow and which are part of the form itself.
If there are restrictions or conditions, insert them here; if not, cross out these words if you wish (see note 3 on the front of this form).

~~subject to the following restrictions and conditions:~~

I intend that this power shall continue even if I become mentally incapable.

I have read or have had read to me the notes in Part A which are part of, and explain, this form.

If this form is being signed at your direction: —
- the person signing must not be an attorney or any witness (to Parts B or C);
- you must add a statement that this form has been signed at your direction;
- a second witness is necessary (please see below).

Your signature (or mark).

Date.

Someone must witness your signature.

Signature of witness.

Your attorney(s) cannot be your witness. It is not advisable for your husband or wife to be your witness.

Signed by me as a deed and delivered   *David P. Ross*

on   10th April 2000

in the presence of   *Thomas Waite*

Full name of witness   Thomas Waite

Address of witness   36 Amber Road

London SW3 5HM

A second witness is only necessary if this form is not being signed by you personally but at your direction (for example, if a physical disability prevents you from signing).

Signature of second witness.

in the presence of

Full name of witness

Address of witness

(Continued on next page)

Completed example of Enduring Power of Attorney (continued)

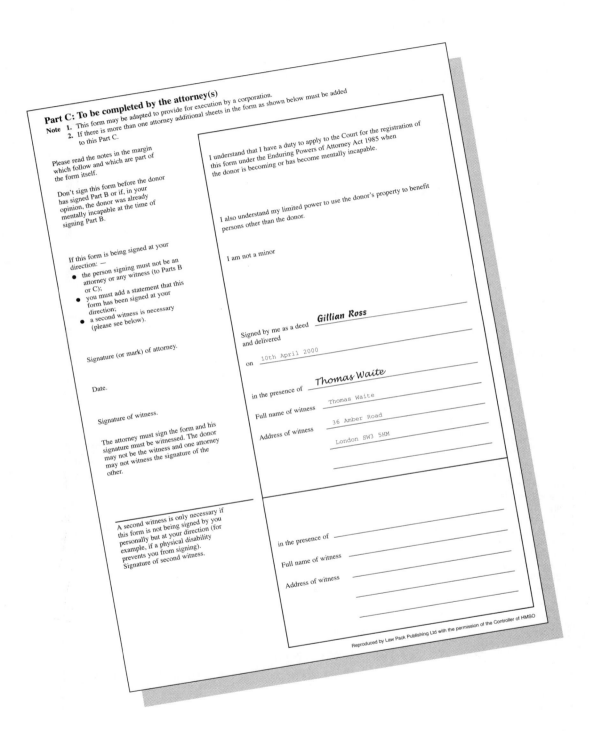

Part C: To be completed by the attorney(s)

Note 1. This form may be adapted to provide for execution by a corporation.
2. If there is more than one attorney additional sheets in the form as shown below must be added to this Part C.

Please read the notes in the margin which follow and which are part of the form itself.

Don't sign this form before the donor has signed Part B or if, in your opinion, the donor was already mentally incapable at the time of signing Part B.

If this form is being signed at your direction: —
- the person signing must not be an attorney or any witness (to Parts B or C);
- you must add a statement that this form has been signed at your direction;
- a second witness is necessary (please see below).

Signature (or mark) of attorney.

Date.

Signature of witness.

The attorney must sign the form and his signature must be witnessed. The donor may not be the witness and one attorney may not witness the signature of the other.

A second witness is only necessary if this form is not being signed by you personally but at your direction (for example, if a physical disability prevents you from signing).
Signature of second witness.

I understand that I have a duty to apply to the Court for the registration of this form under the Enduring Powers of Attorney Act 1985 when the donor is becoming or has become mentally incapable.

I also understand my limited power to use the donor's property to benefit persons other than the donor.

I am not a minor

Signed by me as a deed and delivered   *Gillian Ross*

on   10th April 2000

in the presence of   *Thomas Waite*

Full name of witness   Thomas Waite

Address of witness   36 Amber Road

London SW3 5HM

in the presence of

Full name of witness

Address of witness

Court of Protection/Public Trust Office

Enduring Powers of Attorney Act 1985

Notice of intention to apply for registration

To ....

of..

TAKE NOTICE THAT

This form may be adapted for use by three or more attorneys.

I ....

of ....

and I ....

of ....

Give the name and address of the donor

the attorney(s) of ....

....

of ....

....

intend to apply to the Public Trustee for registration of the enduring power of attorney appointing me (us) attorney(s) and made by the donor on the .... 20........................

It will be necessary for you to produce evidence in support of your objection. If evidence is available please send it with your objection, the attorney(s) will be given an opportunity to respond to your objection.

1. If you wish to object to the proposed registration you have 4 weeks from the day on which this notice is given to you to do so in writing. Any objections should be sent to the Public Trustee and should contain the following details:

   - your name and address;
   - any relationship to the donor;
   - if you are not the donor, the name and address of the donor;
   - the name and address of the attorney;
   - the grounds for objecting to the registration of the enduring power.

The grounds upon which you can object are limited and are shown at 2 overleaf.

EP1

Note. The instrument means the enduring power of attorney made by the donor which it is sought to register.

2. The grounds on which you may object are:

- that the power purported to have been created by the instrument is not valid as an enduring power of attorney;

- that the power created by the instrument no longer subsists;

- that the application is premature because the donor is not yet becoming mentally incapable;

- that fraud or undue pressure was used to induce the donor to make the power;

- that the attorney is unsuitable to be the donor's attorney (having regard to all the circumstances and in particular the attorney's relationship to or connection with the donor).

The attorney(s) does not have to be a relative. Relatives are not entitled to know of the existence of the enduring power of attorney prior to being given this notice.

Note. This is addressed only to the donor.

3. You are informed that while the enduring power of attorney remains registered, you will not be able to revoke it until the Court of Protection confirms the revocation.

Note. This notice should be signed by every one of the attorneys who are applying to register the enduring power of attorney.

Signed .... Dated ....

Signed .... Dated ....

Court of Protection/Public Trust Office, Protection Division, Stewart House, 24 Kingsway, London WC2B 6JX

Completed example of Notice of intention to apply for registration (Form EP1)

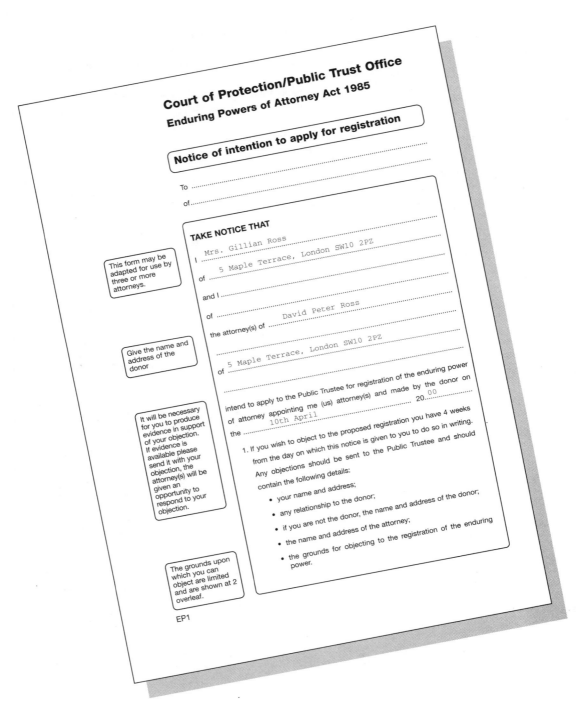

Court of Protection/Public Trust Office
Enduring Powers of Attorney Act 1985

Notice of intention to apply for registration

To ....

of ....

TAKE NOTICE THAT

I Mrs. Gillian Ross ....

of 5 Maple Terrace, London SW10 2PZ ....

and I ....

of David Peter Ross ....

the attorney(s) of ....

5 Maple Terrace, London SW10 2PZ

of ....

intend to apply to the Public Trustee for registration of the enduring power
of attorney appointing me (us) attorney(s) and made by the donor on
the 10th April 20 00

1. If you wish to object to the proposed registration you have 4 weeks
   from the day on which this notice is given to you to do so in writing.
   Any objections should be sent to the Public Trustee and should
   contain the following details:

   - your name and address;
   - any relationship to the donor;
   - if you are not the donor, the name and address of the donor;
   - the name and address of the attorney;
   - the grounds for objecting to the registration of the enduring
     power.

This form may be adapted for use by three or more attorneys.

Give the name and address of the donor

It will be necessary for you to produce evidence in support of your objection. If evidence is available please send it with your objection, the attorney(s) will be given an opportunity to respond to your objection.

The grounds upon which you can object are limited and are shown at 2 overleaf.

EP1

(Continued on next page)

Completed example of Notice of intention to apply for registration (Form EP1) (continued)

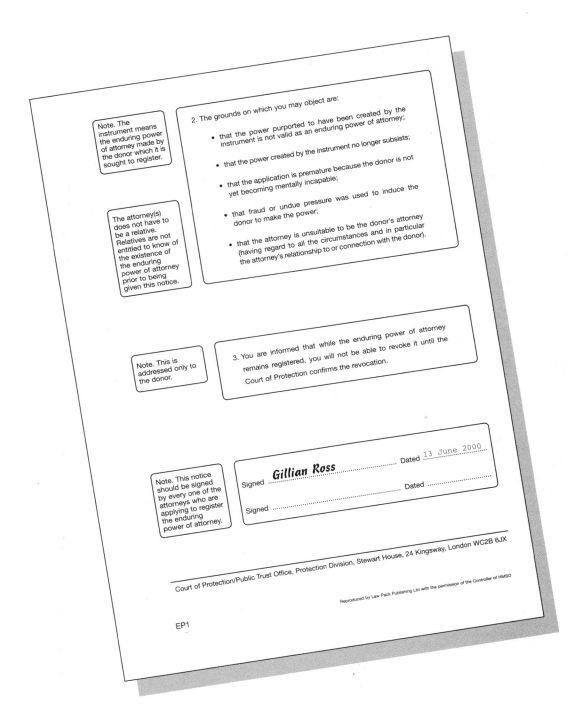

Note. The instrument means the enduring power of attorney made by the donor which it is sought to register.

2. The grounds on which you may object are:

- that the power purported to have been created by the instrument is not valid as an enduring power of attorney;

- that the power created by the instrument no longer subsists;

- that the application is premature because the donor is not yet becoming mentally incapable;

- that fraud or undue pressure was used to induce the donor to make the power;

- that the attorney is unsuitable to be the donor's attorney (having regard to all the circumstances and in particular the attorney's relationship to or connection with the donor).

The attorney(s) does not have to be a relative. Relatives are not entitled to know of the existence of the enduring power of attorney prior to being given this notice.

Note. This is addressed only to the donor.

3. You are informed that while the enduring power of attorney remains registered, you will not be able to revoke it until the Court of Protection confirms the revocation.

Note. This notice should be signed by every one of the attorneys who are applying to register the enduring power of attorney.

Signed *Gillian Ross* .... Dated 13 June 2000

Signed .... Dated ....

Court of Protection/Public Trust Office, Protection Division, Stewart House, 24 Kingsway, London WC2B 6JX

Reproduced by Law Pack Publishing Ltd with the permission of the Controller of HMSO

EP1

No. _____

Court of Protection/Public Trust Office

Enduring Powers of Attorney Act 1985

Application for registration

Note. Give the full name and present address of the donor. If the donor's address on the enduring power of attorney is different give that one too.

The donor

Name ....

Address ....

....

Address on the Enduring Power of Attorney (if different) ....

....

Note. Give the full name(s) and details of the attorney(s).

The attorney(s)

Name ....

Address ....

age.............................. occupation...

relationship to donor (if any) ....

Name ....

Address ....

age.............................. occupation...

relationship to donor (if any) ....

This form may be adapted for use by three of more attorneys.

The date is the date upon which the donor signed the enduring power of attorney.

I (we) the attorney(s) apply to register the enduring power of attorney made by the donor under the above Act on

the .... 20.....................

the original of which accompanies this application.

I (we) have reason to believe that the donor is or is becoming mentally incapable.

Notice must be personally given. It should be made clear if someone other than the attorney(s) gives the notice.

I (we) have given notice in the prescribed form to the following:

- the donor personally at ....

....

on the .... 20.....................

EP2

- The following relatives of the donor at the addresses below on the dates given:

Names	Relationship	Addresses	Date

- The Co-Attorney(s) ....

  at ....

  on ....

A remittance for the registration fee accompanies this application.

I (we) certify that the above information is correct and that to the best of my (our) knowledge and belief I (we) have complied with the provisions of the Enduring Powers of Attorney Act 1985 and of all the Rules and Regulations under it.

Signed .... Dated ....

Signed .... Dated ....

....

Address to which correspondence relating to the application is to be sent if different to that of the first-named attorney making this application

....

....

When completed this form should be sent to:–
Court of Protection/Public Trust Office, Protection Division, Stewart House, 24 Kingsway, London WC2B 6JX

EP2

Completed example of Application for registration (Form EP2)

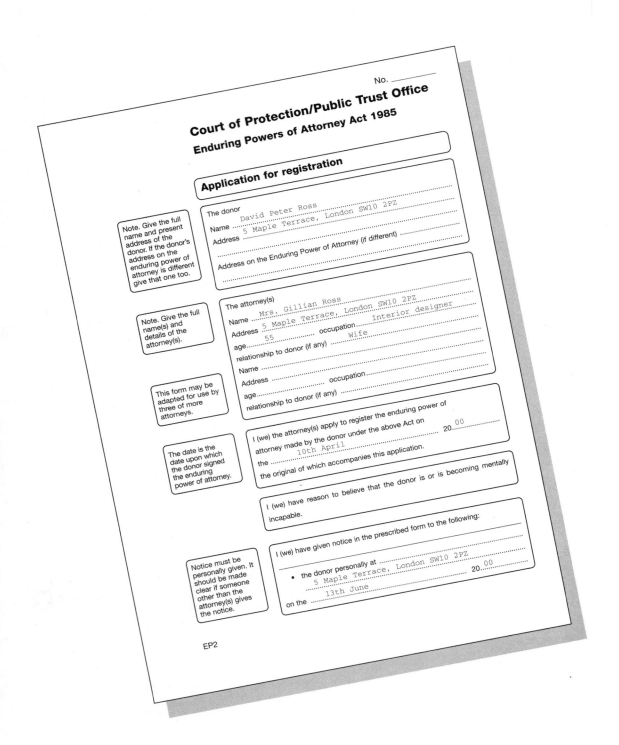

No. _____

Court of Protection/Public Trust Office
Enduring Powers of Attorney Act 1985

Application for registration

Note. Give the full name and present address of the donor. If the donor's address on the enduring power of attorney is different give that one too.

The donor

Name   David Peter Ross

Address   5 Maple Terrace, London SW10 2PZ

Address on the Enduring Power of Attorney (if different)

Note. Give the full name(s) and details of the attorney(s).

The attorney(s)

Name   Mrs. Gillian Ross

Address   5 Maple Terrace, London SW10 2PZ

age   55   occupation   Interior designer

relationship to donor (if any)   Wife

Name

Address   occupation

age

relationship to donor (if any)

This form may be adapted for use by three of more attorneys.

The date is the date upon which the donor signed the enduring power of attorney.

I (we) the attorney(s) apply to register the enduring power of attorney made by the donor under the above Act on

the   10th April   20 00

the original of which accompanies this application.

I (we) have reason to believe that the donor is or is becoming mentally incapable.

I (we) have given notice in the prescribed form to the following:

Notice must be personally given. It should be made clear if someone other than the attorney(s) gives the notice.

• the donor personally at   5 Maple Terrace, London SW10 2PZ

on the   13th June   20 00

EP2

(Continued on next page)

Completed example of Application for registration (Form EP2) (continued)

- The following relatives of the donor at the addresses below on the dates given:

Names	Relationship	Addresses	Date
			14-6-00
Susanna Hill	Sister	90 Dorset Mansions London W14	14-6-00
Nigel Ross	Brother	32 Church Grove London SW6	14-6-00
Richard Ross	Father	7 Kings Walk Leamington LM9	14-6-00
Mary Jane Ross	Daughter	62 Jagger Road London SW11	

If there are no relatives entitled to notice please say so.

Note. Cross out this section if it does not apply.

- The Co-Attorney(s) ....

at ....

on ....

A remittance for the registration fee accompanies this application.

I (we) certify that the above information is correct and that to the best of my (our) knowledge and belief I (we) have complied with the provisions of the Enduring Powers of Attorney Act 1985 and of all the Rules and Regulations under it.

Note. The application should be signed by all the attorneys who are making the application.

.... Dated 19 August 2000

Signed ....

Signed .... Dated ....

....

This must not pre-date the date(s) when the notices were given.

Address to which correspondence relating to the application is to be sent if different to that of the first-named attorney making this application

....

....

When completed this form should be sent to:–

Court of Protection/Public Trust Office, Protection Division, Stewart House, 24 Kingsway, London WC2B 6JX

Reproduced by Law Pack Publishing Ltd with the permission of the Controller of HMSO

EP2

Court of Protection/Public Trust Office

Enduring Powers of Attorney Act 1985
In the matter of a power given by

.... (a donor)

to ....(attorney)

and ....(attorney)

If this application is being made prior to an application for registration the original enduring power of attorney should accompany this application.

General form of application

I ....

of ....

and I ....

of ....

Apply for an order or directions that ....

....

....

....

....

....

and for any other directions which are necessary as a result of my/our application.

The grounds on which I/we make this applications are:

....

....

....

....

Note. Give details of the order or directions that you are seeking.

State under which sub-section of the Enduring Powers of Attorney Act 1985 or which rule of the Court of Protection (Enduring Powers of Attorney) Rules 1994 this application is made.

Note. Give details of the grounds on which you are seeking the order or directions.

Evidence in support should accompany this application.

Signed .... Dated..................

Signed .... Dated..................

Address where notices should be sent ....

....

....

Note. The application should be signed by all the applicants or their solicitors.

When completed this form should be sent to:–

Court of Protection/Public Trust Office, Protection Division, Stewart House, 24 Kingsway, London WC2B 6JX

Completed example of General form of application (Form EP3)

Court of Protection/Public Trust Office

Enduring Powers of Attorney Act 1985

In the matter of a power given by

.... David Peter Ross .... (a donor)

to .... Gillian Ross .... (attorney)

and .... (attorney)

General form of application

> *If this application is being made prior to an application for registration the original enduring power of attorney should accompany this application.*

I, Gillian Ross

of 5 Maple Terrace, London SW10 2PZ

and I ....

of ....

Apply for an order or directions that I be permanently appointed to handle the affairs of David Peter Ross as his attorney under an Enduring Power of Attorney dated 10 April 2000

....

and for any other directions which are necessary as a result of my/our application.

The grounds on which I/we make this applications are:
That the donor has become mentally incapable to handle his own affairs

....

> *Note. Give details of the order or directions that you are seeking.*

> *State under which sub-section of the Enduring Powers of Attorney Act 1985 or which rule of the Court of Protection (Enduring Powers of Attorney) Rules 1994 this application is made.*

> *Note. Give details of the grounds on which you are seeking the order or directions.*

> *Evidence in support should accompany this application.*

Dated 10-6-2000

Signed ....   Dated ....

Signed ....

Address where notices should be sent ....
5 Maple Terrace, London SW10 2PZ

> *Note. The application should be signed by all the applicants or their solicitors.*

When completed this form should be sent to:–
Court of Protection/Public Trust Office, Protection Division, Stewart House, 24 Kingsway, London WC2B 6JX

Reproduced by Law Pack Publishing Ltd with the permission of the Controller of HMSO

EP3

GENERAL POWER OF ATTORNEY
(Pursuant to the Powers of Attorney Act 1971, section 10)

THIS GENERAL POWER OF ATTORNEY is made

this_____ day of _____ 20 _____

BY   _____

    OF   _____

            _____

I APPOINT

            _____

            _____

[jointly][jointly and severally] to be my attorney(s) in accordance with section 10 of the Powers of Attorney Act 1971.

IN WITNESS whereof I have hereunto set my hand the day and year first above written.

SIGNED as a Deed and Delivered by the

       said   _____

       in the presence of _____

Completed example of General Power of Attorney

GENERAL POWER OF ATTORNEY
(Pursuant to the Powers of Attorney Act 1971, section 10)

THIS GENERAL POWER OF ATTORNEY is made

this 3rd day of ___July___ 20 00

BY   Matthew James Ross

OF   52 Artillery Street, London E13 7SL

I APPOINT   Jonathan Edward Spencer of 22 Maple Terrace, London SW10 7XA

and Sarah Jane Spencer of 22 Maple Terrace, London SW10 7XA

[jointly][jointly and severally] to be my attorney(s) in accordance with section 10 of the Powers of Attorney Act 1971.

IN WITNESS whereof I have hereunto set my hand the day and year first above written.

SIGNED as a Deed and Delivered by the

said   *MJ Ross*

in the presence of   *Andrew Kennington*

LIVING WILL

Name_____

Address_____

Date of Birth_____

Doctor's details_____

National Health Number_____

I, _____, am of sound mind and make this Advance Directive now on my future medical care to my family, my doctors, other medical personnel and anyone else to whom it is relevant, for a time when, for reasons of physical or mental incapacity, I am unable to make my views known.

INSTRUCTIONS

Medical treatment I DO NOT want

I REFUSE medical procedures to prolong my life or keep me alive by artificial means if:-

(1) I have a severe physical illness from which, in the opinion of _____ independent medical practitioners, it is unlikely that I will ever recover;   ☐

or

(2) I have a severe mental illness which, in the opinion of _____ independent medical practitioners, has no likelihood of improvement and in addition I have a severe physical illness from which, in the opinion of _____ independent medical practitioners, it is unlikely that I will ever recover;   ☐

or

(3) I am permanently unconscious and have been so for a period of at least ____ months and in the opinion of two independent medical practitioners there is no likelihood that I will ever recover.   ☐

Medical treatment I DO want

I DO wish to receive any medical treatment which will alleviate pain or distressing symptoms or will make me more comfortable. I accept that this may have the effect of shortening my life.   ☐

[If I am suffering from any of the conditions above and I am pregnant, I wish to RECEIVE medical procedures which will prolong my life or keep me alive by artificial means only until such time as my child has been safely delivered.]

HEALTH CARE PROXY

I wish to appoint _____ of _____
_____ as my Health Care
Proxy. S/he should be involved in any decisions about my health care options if I am physically or
mentally unable to make my views known. I wish to make it clear that s/he is fully aware of my
wishes and I request that his/her decisions be respected.

ADDITIONAL DIRECTIONS ON FUTURE HEALTH CARE

_____
_____
_____
_____
_____
_____
_____
_____

SIGNATURES

Signature _____ Date _____

Witness' Signature _____ Date _____

I confirm that my views are still as stated above.

	Date	Signature	Witness' Signature
1)			
2)			
3)			
4)			

Completed example of Living Will

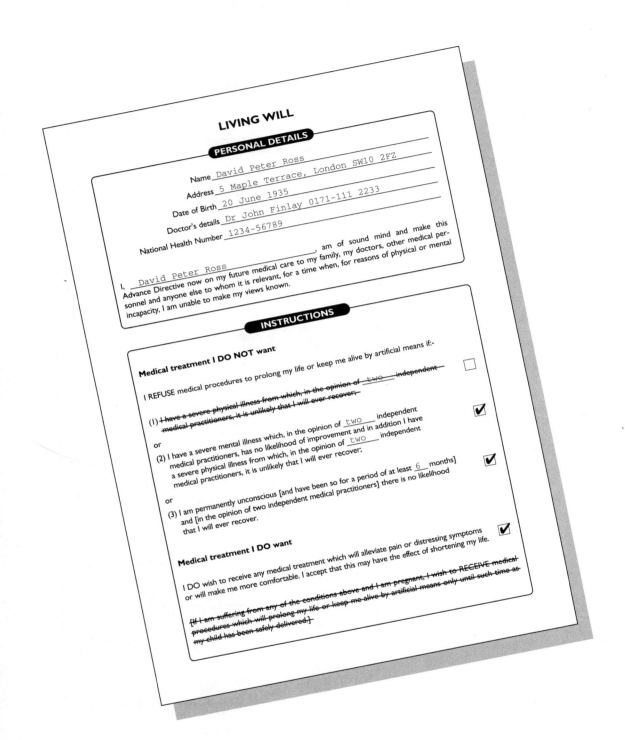

LIVING WILL

PERSONAL DETAILS

Name David Peter Ross

Address 5 Maple Terrace, London SW10 2FZ

Date of Birth 20 June 1935

Doctor's details Dr John Finlay 0171-111 2233

National Health Number 1234-56789

I, David Peter Ross , am of sound mind and make this Advance Directive now on my future medical care to my family, my doctors, other medical personnel and anyone else to whom it is relevant, for a time when, for reasons of physical or mental incapacity, I am unable to make my views known.

INSTRUCTIONS

Medical treatment I DO NOT want

I REFUSE medical procedures to prolong my life or keep me alive by artificial means if:- ☐

(1) I have a severe physical illness from which, in the opinion of ~~two~~ ~~independent medical practitioners, it is unlikely that I will ever recover;~~

or

(2) I have a severe mental illness which, in the opinion of two independent medical practitioners, has no likelihood of improvement and in addition I have a severe physical illness from which, in the opinion of two independent medical practitioners, it is unlikely that I will ever recover; ☑

or

(3) I am permanently unconscious [and have been so for a period of at least 6 months] and [in the opinion of two independent medical practitioners] there is no likelihood that I will ever recover. ☑

Medical treatment I DO want

I DO wish to receive any medical treatment which will alleviate pain or distressing symptoms or will make me more comfortable. I accept that this may have the effect of shortening my life. ☑

~~[If I am suffering from any of the conditions above and I am pregnant, I wish to RECEIVE medical procedures which will prolong my life or keep me alive by artificial means only until such time as my child has been safely delivered.]~~

(Continued on next page)

Completed example of Living Will (continued)

HEALTH CARE PROXY

I wish to appoint ___Mrs. Gillian Ross___ of ___ as my Health Care
___5 Maple Terrace, London SW10 2FZ___
Proxy. S/he should be involved in any decisions about my health care options if I am physically or
mentally unable to make my views known. I wish to make it clear that s/he is fully aware of my
wishes and I request that his/her decisions are respected.

ADDITIONAL DIRECTIONS ON FUTURE HEALTH CARE

___None___

SIGNATURES

Signature ___David Ross___ Date ___10 April 2000___

Witness' Signature ___Thomas Waite___ Date ___10 April 2000___

I confirm that my views are still as stated above.

Date	Signature	Witness' Signature
1)		
2)		
3)		
4)		

Index

Notes

Notes

Notes

Notes

Notes

More books and software from Law Pack...

Law Pack **Form Books** are invaluable storehouses of literally hundreds of ready-made legal and business documents, for use at work or at home.

Law Pack **Guides** are user-friendly, do-it-yourself manuals that take the reader step by step through a specific subject and its procedures. Information, instructions and advice are backed up with example paperwork for guidance.

Home & Family Solicitor

The essential do-it-yourself legal resource for every home. From taking action against a noisy neighbour to drawing up a live-in nanny's employment contract, this Form Book will provide you with the ideal, ready-to-use legal letter or agreement. Covers: Credit & Finance, Employment, Goods, Services & Utilities, Insurance, Personal & Family, Lettings & Property, Local Environment.

301 Legal Forms, Letters & Agreements

Our **best-selling Form Book now in its fifth edition**. It is packed with forms, letters and agreements for legal protection in virtually every situation. It provides a complete do-it-yourself library of 301 ready-to-use legal documents, for business or personal use. Areas covered include Loans & Borrowing, Buying & Selling, Employment, Transfers & Assignments and Tenancy.

User testimonials on *301 Legal Forms, Letters & Agreements*:

'A long awaited and needed publication which is a handy reference guide for almost every occurrence'
Ms R G Jones, Bank Officer, Gillingham, Kent.

'Absolutely brilliant. Would be lost without it. Ideal for any business'
Richard Shaw, Company Director, Leeds.

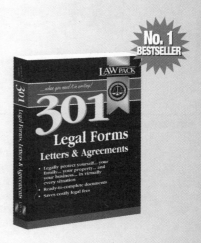

Code B418 • ISBN 1 902646 18 5 • A4 PB
192 pp • £19.99 • 2nd Edition

Code B402 • ISBN 1 902646 72 X • A4 PB
358 pp • £19.99 • 7th Edition

... to order, simply call 020 7940 7000 or visit www.lawpack.co.uk

Limited Company

Do you want to set up a business? This Guide explains how to set up your own limited company yourself. It is packed with explanations of procedure, and includes examples of Companies House forms, Memorandum and Articles of Association, resolutions and provides answers to all questions. Valid in England and Wales, and Scotland.

Code B405 • ISBN 1 902646 58 4 • 246 x 189mm PB
96 pp • £9.99 • 3rd Edition

Small Claims

If you want to take action to recover a debt, resolve a contract dispute or make a personal injury claim, you can file your own small claim without a solicitor. This Guide includes clear instructions and advice on how to handle your own case and enforce judgment.

Code B406 • ISBN 1 902646 04 5 • A4 PB
96 pp • £9.99 • 2nd Edition

Employment Law

Whether you are an employer or an employee, you have rights in the workplace. This best-selling Guide is a comprehensive reference source on hiring, wages, employment contracts, termination, discrimination and other important issues. It puts at your fingertips all the important legal points employers and employees should know.

Code B408 • ISBN 1 902646 24 X • 246 x 189mm PB
148 pp • £9.99 • 4th Edition

... to order, simply call 020 7940 7000 or visit www.lawpack.co.uk

Probate

What happens when someone dies, with or without leaving a Will, and their estate needs to be dealt with? Probate is the process whereby the deceased's executors apply for authority to handle the deceased's assets. This Guide provides the information and instructions needed to obtain a grant of probate, or grant of letters of administration, and administer an estate without the expense of a solicitor.

Code B409 • ISBN 1 902646 27 4 • 246 x 189mm PB
110 pp • £9.99 • 2nd Edition

Divorce

File your own undefended divorce and save legal fees! This Guide explains the process from filing your petition to final decree. Even if there are complications such as young children or contested grounds this Guide will save you time and money.

Code B404 • ISBN 1 902646 05 3 • A4 PB
120 pp • £9.99 • 2nd Edition

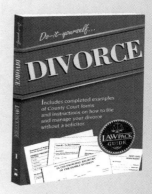

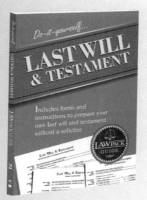

Last Will & Testament

With the help of this Guide writing a Will can be a straightforward matter. It takes the reader step by step through the process of drawing up a Will, while providing background information and advice. Will forms, completed examples and checklists included.

Code B403 • ISBN 1 902646 06 1 • A4 PB
80 pp • £9.99 • 2nd Edition

... to order, simply call 020 7940 7000 or visit www.lawpack.co.uk

Motoring Law

Whether we like it or not, motoring is fact of everyday life. But how many drivers actually know their rights and those of the police? The Highway Code provides the driving basics. This Law Pack Guide is essential follow-up reading on the motorist's real rights and remedies.

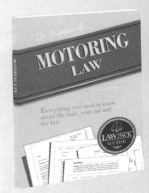

Code B415 • ISBN 1 898217 51 3 • A4 PB
104 pp • £9.99 • 1st Edition

Credit File

Refused credit? Bad credit? We nearly all rely on credit, whether it be with the bank, mortgage lender or credit card company. This Law Pack Guide explains just how credit agencies work, what goes on to your credit file and what legitimate action you can take to improve it. It divulges lenders decision-making processes and blows the lid off 'credit repair' and credit 'blacklists'.

Code B413 • ISBN 1 898217 77 7 • A4 pb
76 pp • £9.99 • 1st Edition

House Buying, Selling and Conveyancing

It isn't true that only those who have gone through long, expensive and involved training can possibly understand the intricacies of house buying, selling and conveyancing. This Law Pack Guide is a new, updated edition of a best-selling book by Joseph Bradshaw, once described in *The Times* as the 'guru of layperson conveyancing', which explains step-by-step just how straightforward the whole process really is. Required reading for all house buyers (or sellers).

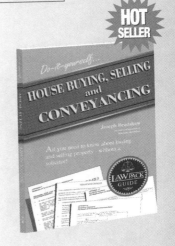

Code B412 • ISBN 1 898712 72 6 • A4 PB
192pp • £9.99 • 1st Edition

... to order, simply call 020 7940 7000 or visit www.lawpack.co.uk

Law Pack Legal Adviser

Fast answers to nearly all your legal questions! The *Law Pack Legal Adviser* is a comprehensive and succinct guide on the different ways the law influences our everyday lives. It covers such topics as setting up home, children, work, buying goods and services, neighbours, sports, holidays, motoring, money, the police, and the legal system. *Legal Adviser* is a clear and reliable guide to one's rights under the law and is as essential in the home as any standard reference book.

Code B421 • ISBN 1 902646 53 3 • 246 x189mm PB
300pp • £14.99

Cohabitation Rights

As more couples choose not to marry, the legal and financial issues they face with children, mortgages, pensions, separation and death become ever more important to understand and address. This book discusses the options in cohabitation agreements, and provides practical advice for couples.

Code B423 • ISBN 1 902646 52 5 • 246 x 189mm PB
150pp • £9.99

Residential Lettings

Required reading for anyone letting residential property. Covering the legal background and including real-life case studies, this book provides all that a would-be landlord needs to know before letting a flat or house. It covers preparation of the property, finding a tenant, the tenancy agreement, problem tenants, buy-to-let, HMOs and more.

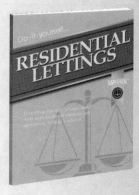

Code B422 • ISBN 1 902646 51 7 • 246 x 189mm PB
150pp • £9.99